I0519039

GUNK

Noah David Roberts

QUERENCIA

Querencia Press – Chicago IL

QUERENCIA PRESS

© Copyright 2024
Noah David Roberts

All Rights Reserved

No reproduction, copy or transmission of this publication may be made
without written permission.
No paragraph of this publication may be reproduced, copied, or transmitted
save with the written permission of the author.

Any person who commits any unauthorized act in relation to this publication
may be liable to criminal prosecution and civil claims for damages.

ISBN 978 1 959118 89 3

.

www.querenciapress.com

First Published in 2024

Querencia Press, LLC
Chicago IL

Printed & Bound in the United States of America

GUNK

PRELUDE

Before We Eat the Rat
   —after Dorothea Lasky

Cacophony sleeps, derelict,
deranged. Empty head. Dip the rat
completely in oil. You want to, don't you.

My mother's voice shakes walls.
It's in my hands, slipping. Aerosol cans
& spatulas. Slick, sleek explosives

taped to underside of flatbed.
Detonator, rat. I hold in my hands a
remote control deity. Dip the rat

in oil, glistening with oil. I want you to.
I've thrown up on the golden rug.
Hold, tightly. Sleep in sweat with

white moonlight peeking through.
Water crackles when it touches hot oil,
wiping my oily mouth on the quilt

I did not inherit. I drool, consuming.
I don't want to dip the rat in oil. Meek
whimper, bleating whine. Any mammal would

drown celebrated when the oil
enters its nostrils. Because you told me,
I drop the rat in & fry it, scrambling, alive.

SINLESS

1: BIRTH

I WAKE DRIPPING WITH IT
THE LOCKS WET THE DOOR JAMMED
THE JAM SPREAD THE DRAPES TOUCH
THE FLOOR SOMEONE'S BEEN HERE

I THINK BUT NOT REALLY BECAUSE
THERE ISN'T A PLACE FOR YOU
TO HIDE ANYMORE LIKE I WAKE DRIPPING
WITH IT LIKE I WAKE DRIPPING WITHOUT IT

A GUNMETAL CLOUD IN THE SKY LIKE
I USED TO HAVE TO TREASURE IT LIKE
I WAKE DRIPPING WITHOUT YOU
I WAKE DRIPPING WITHOUT YOU

I WAKE DRIPPING WITHOUT YOU
I WAKE KNOWING NOTHING

2: DAY

I WAKE KNOWING NOTHING
IN THE MORNING I AM REAL
IN THE MORNING I AM REAL
I SHAKE MY OWN HANDS
CONCUSSIONS CAUSE THE BRAIN TO
MOVE FROM SIDE TO SIDE BUT

I MOVE FROM DARK TO DARK A
BEAST OF RAINBOW BEING & CLEAR
ENTITY YOU CAN SEE THROUGH
MY PRETTY MOUTH A SMILE OF TEETH
GROWING INTO OBLIVION LIPSTICK KISS
SMOKING IN A BACK LOT PARKING GARAGE
SHINING A STEEL FLASHLIGHT UPON
A DRENCHING DARKENED LIMPING STORM

3: STORM

A DRENCHING DARKENED LIMPING STORM
STRIKES DOWN UPON THE SKIN A
TREE BLACKENED BY LIGHTNING FLAME
LEAVES SOIL RICH & ASHEN
STEP INTO THE MUD DROP YOUR
BODY IN THE MUD THROW THOUGHTS
INTO THE MUD IT TURNS TO TAR
BLACKTOP ON A HOT DAY MELTING
& DESOLATION IS A FORM OF GUNK
GROWING IN THE DESERT WHEN IT RAINS
ROTTEN ACACIA STRAINING THROUGH ARID
SLOP WHICH IS ROTTING APPLE'S SLUDGE
NEW YORK HAS MY BIRTH IN BROWNED SNOW
VOMIT HITS THE FLOOR SO THERE IS FEAR

4: NIGHT

VOMIT HITS THE FLOOR THERE IS FEAR
OR DISEASE FECKLESS LUNG COUGHS COUGHS

BROWN TAR BROWN TAR BROWN TAR BROWN TAR
MY BODY IS DISGUSTING & I AM MADE OF SHIT BUT

HALO ADORNS MY BROKEN SKULL A VEIL UPON
MY SHATTERED BONES A VINYL BAG A BURLAP SACK

HEY DEVIL I SEE YOU NOW YOUR BROKEN LIP
YOUR DROOL HANGING LOW YOUR SHARPENED TOOTH

I AM NOT AFRAID OF THE UNREAL LIKE YOUR WINGS CARRY US
OVER THE FIRE INTO LAKES OF HARD ICE

GAUNT BODY HAUNTING A NATURE AROUND MY DAUNT
-ING SCARE LIKE THE UTMOST OF THE WORLD

WET CLUMPS OF HACKSAW HAIR ON THE
DRAIN OF THE WORLD ECHOING SOLACE

5: SOLACE

DRAIN OF THE WORLD ECHOING SOLACE

I COME TO YOU TONIGHT IN MOURNING IN

A LONG DARK DRESS TO IMITATE THAT STORM

-Y SMOKE EYESHADOW UPON A BROKEN FACE

EXCEPT FOR A TONGUE IN A PRETTY MOUTH

MY UGLY MOUTH OF BROKEN YELLOW TEETH

GROWING OLD GROWING OLD GROWING OLD

ROTTING GUNK OF ME ROTTING GUNK OF ME

MIRROR GLANCING OFF OF SUNLIGHT

THE RISING STARS KEEP THEIR SECRETS

I WAIT TO KILL I WAIT TO KILL WHO I THOUGHT

DRAINED THE WORLD OF ECHOING SOLACE

I WAKE DRIPPING WITH IT

GUNK
          —*after Joy Division*

When will it end this absurd decomposition

lifting from empty floors
from empty floors
                    hollow door

when will it end when will it end
this absurd decomposition
hypnosis, emptiness, melting, drown
                                        -ing
                hollow
        door

hollow door hollow door full of gunk
excrement dying excrement dying
excrement dying excrement dying

I feel like shit & my ribs are broken
my ribs are broken & beating
your skull against the hollow

never got us anywhere when will
it end when will it end

DEFAULT STATE: PARANOIA

DESOLATE CONTAINED ATARAXIC METASTASIZING UBIQUITY
BORES DOWN MY EYELIDS & CRADLES THROUGH TO
MY CORNEAS & BURNS ME BLIND. A CHILD I WAS WHEN LAST
I SAW YOU. BUT WHEN YOU LAST SAW ME IT WAS UNDER THE GUN
-KINESS. NATURE OF THE SKY IS PASTEL STOLEN SILK. A NATURE
SEEPED IN GASOLINE. DIESEL OIL THE HARD STUFF SINKING INTO
THE GROUND BELOW & TRANSFORMING. GUNK OF MY EYE,
OF DAYS I LIVED IN NEW YORK. I SAW PEOPLE IN THE WALLS
WIGGLING BENEATH WOODEN WALLPAPER & I HAVE NEVER
HAD A REFLECTION. THERE IS NO FACE TO ME BUT I RECOGNIZE.
NOW YOU ARE HERE TO KILL. I WAS HEALED, FOR A WHILE
BUT HEALING IS ACTIVE & HATING IS PASSIVE. I AM HATE
IN THE UGLY BLOOD THAT GUNKS THE DRAINS, THE
GUTTERS, ARTERIES. IN THE BASEMENT APARTMENT
I FOUND GOD, HIDING WITH A BLEAK SNAKE-SKIN UNDER
THE KITCHEN COUNTER, DUSTED WITH APHASIA &
EXPHRASIS. IN MY HOME I BUILT A WEAPON
MADE OF RUSTED PINS & GRAVEL, PREPARED TO USE.
AN INSULT JUST DOESN'T CUT AS DEEP
ANYMORE I NEED TO TASTE THE IRON & SHIELD
WITH THE TEETH I BROKE ON CONCRETE, PORCELAIN
FALLING INTO PUDDLES OF MUD &
DANCING SCATTERED TO THE STREETLINES.

SNAKE

Backing its way down the stairs / stretching its back / along the stairs / elongated python / which doesn't scare me anymore / I just know it is there at all times / long neck & head & tongue hovering above / I don't talk & the python doesn't either / & my floorboards make screaming sounds when I feel sort of bad / or worse / the python enters my sleep / & I see you / & you are the closest thing to the python that I will love / I feel like I fucked up my twenties by the way / there's a dirty glass at the bottom of my sink / sank with bubbles of stinking soap / snake tongue tells all anyway / acidic like grief / stands / at the top of the stairwell / tightening a glove / dispersing into shadow with the python / to the python apocalypse means to reveal a secret / to me it means saying what I need to say

CANDIED APPLES

DANCE WITH ME YOUR LEGS ARE WATERY & COLD. EPOCH OF HELL. EPOCH EPOCH WITH JEALOUSY IN MIND. MY VULNERABILITY IS INTERRUPTED BY THIS BRIEF ADVERTISEMENT; IT IS TIME TO PURCHASE YOUR INIMITABLE TREASURE WHICH, MUCH LIKE YOURSELF, IS UNDERWHELMING. YOUR LOVE IS SUPREME & THERE IS NOTHING YOU CAN DO ABOUT IT, YOUR HARROW & BLEAKNESS JUSTIFIED IN THE ENDLESS TRAGEDY OF LIVING. EPOCH WHICH LOST ITS MIND LOST YOUR MIND LOST MY MIND. TEMPORALITY IS MYTHOLOGICAL IN THE MODERN AGE OF CANDIED APPLES. THERE IS A SADNESS IN YOU THAT YOU CAN'T GET OUT OR IN OTHER WORDS A HALLWAY IN A DOORJAMB THAT WASN'T THERE BEFORE. THE MIST & ZONE TELL YOU OTHERWISE, PLAY TRICKS. IT'S FUCKING WITH YOU. IT'S YOUR PRIDE, MAN, YOU GOT NOTHING ELSE TO LIVE FOR THAN THIS, HANDLING THE CANDY & FRUIT, DIP THE FRUIT IN CANDIED SUGAR. DISPLACEMENT LIKE TREPIDATIOUS AXIOM IN THE EPOCH OF MY OWN MAKING. TRANCE LIKE YOU MEAN IT, LIE IN PILES OF HEATED SUGAR WHICH IN TIME TRANSFORMS TO GUNK & INVADES YOUR PORES EYES EARS MOUTH UNDER YOUR FINGERNAILS THERE IS THE GUNK OF A THOUSAND ROTTING CANDIED APPLES YOU ARE HORRIFIED AT THE SIGHTS BEFORE YOU BUT YOU LOVE IT & EAT THEM ALL THE SAME, DROOL HANGING FROM YOUR MOSQUITO MOUTH.

A LITTLE BIRD (FUNERARY)

What the mountain has awakened within us is
a trepidatious uncanniness. Summertime was
nervous breakdown after nervous breakdown.
Red goats, mosquitoes, terrified skin, trust
the breaking-apart-ness, I feel the need to put down
what has been told to me as I scratch the final resting
place of the tendons in my arms, they rest upon your chest—
without severing, I remove the veins from my wrists

        & tie them in knots around the parts of you I love.
        Without faltering or fault, I weather my whetstone
        with dense gunk. It is raw so it is sure to sharpen the
        stone. I tie my knots & rest assured, this treasure is

    like psychosis ending. Heal the parts of you that are
    lacerated by infinity, by treasured apathetic milieu.
    Mountain stands, streets run before me. A desperation,
    a long trench full of fuchsia petals, gaunt & gelid. It is
    the long place between seasons, & your bare feet
    stand upon glass petals, grass shards which,
    like nettles, pierce the parts of you that are vulnerable.

My place in this world has become a window,
I believe I have psychic powers, embody all
that is gestating in my gut, power through
fungus & heartache & fire & sword & swarms
of ugly insects which pass around plague
like bottles, a jaw broken in muddy pastoral.

QUINTET FOR SHOUTING

TO ANY ENTITY WHICH HOVERS HUMMING
  THE TUNE TO CHOPIN'S *NOCTURNE IN C SHARP MINOR*
TO ANY ENTITY LEFT FOR DEAD UNDER A RED SKY
  FULL OF ASH & SOOT
TO ANY AUTUMNAL NIGHT FULL OF RAIN

TO A RAINY SEPTEMBER NIGHT WHEN
  THE EYES IN THE SKY ARE BLINKING DOWNERS
  TRAILBLAZING YOUR INKBLOT SHIFTING IN THE NIGHT
TO THE THOUGHT OF DEATH PERISHING IN NIGHT
TO LIGHTNING INVOCATIONS I INVOKE LIGHT

FROM MY PRETTY MOUTH I INVOKE LIGHT
LIPSTICK ON THE WINDOW OF A SOUTHBOUND BUS
  I INVOKE LIGHT
MY LIFE SAVINGS IS A BUCKET OF QUARTERS
  & I INVOKE LIGHT TO

INVOKE LIGHT I MUST FIRST BE IN DARK
SO IN BECOMING ATMOSPHERE'S CURVE
  I BREATHE THE SAME SMOKE YOU BREATHE
SO IN BECOMING OPAQUE I BECOME
  MY MOST VULNERABLE

SO IN BECOMING I AM ALWAYS BECOMING SOMETHING ELSE
  I AM NO LONGER AFRAID A BROKEN HOLLOW DOOR
  TRANCE TRANCE HYPNOTIZE ME LIKE SPINNING WHEELS
IT WAS A MERCILESS SUMMER OR TO SAY THE SAME THING AGAIN
  A NECK WITH AN AXE-BLADE, GLEAMING.

BONES WRAPPED IN BURLAP

Nothing to be human smudge
in your bones & marrow
  petrified sludge
of slop humanity
destiny of pigs of ruin or
in other words,
  misery working
its claws under a shoulderblade
which in a fury explodes
a spine of its own my
  perception of
a hollow door is trancing
licking together paper wounds
sending away its letters
  I remember my
father would always say
prepare for the best
expect the worst
  this is probably why
I always leave my windows
open that hollow door
lacks what I think is not there
  shadow gnarling twist
-ing spinal cord double-helix
I am still intestinal
locked within this centrifuge
  maladaption makes me
delirious. Sometimes we return
veiled thing your hood is dark
-ening in the rain

slow lips upon my watery
eye are a grazing lash
release into me your warmth
as this devastation is ongoing
I lie my body down
in the river & drift on effusion
to breathe under that dark rain
I administer to my body a strain
of highly noxious mold
it is sure to kill me quick
so before it does,
kiss my body, a ribcage made of burlap.

DIGGING

Lack is the standard definition of a hole. A great big hole in the street. Pothole, sinkhole, fault lines. Bellybuttons & ear piercings, tiny holes left by needles. Black spot, history of hole symbolism. Black hole I can never photograph. Holes where my eyes should be. Dead & empty holes! Wet slop holes of mud in my backyard, I remember falling when I was younger. Dirty holes! Hole in the wall hole in the ground. Body holes, plot holes, bullet holes, crochet. Trypophobia, foam bubbles look like holes when they are fine enough. My heart a place I'd love to have a hole. Oh how I witness even with two empty eye-holes, oh how I hear with my ear-holes. Holes in my face allow breath & consumption. Blood comes from more holes than it doesn't. Put your holes into me, together we are a big, dark, stinking hole, together we devour; although sometimes I wonder if I can tell you who is devourer/devoured. A long trench is just an elongated hole. Rifles have holes. Targets have holes. Aim for the hole, you know what I mean (golf). Like when I accidentally let loose an arrow & left a hole in your tire. My whole life is a hole. Hole to fall down into. Grave-hole, death-hole. Shovels are not how to dig this hole. You must denigrate & depreciate to enjoy your fullest hole-ness. I leave holes everywhere I go, daily affirmation. I am one of many holes left behind. Beyond the hole is only more hole. Look within the hole to find the hole, etc. Boy do I love holes. Anything could be down in that hole. Hope for treasure in the hole, not fire. I peer into the hole & see no bones. See, the hole never had a body anyway. The hole never thought, I am a hole—I don't think. Maybe it did. Maybe the hole knows it's a hole, & is doing what I am doing, refracted, upside-down, mirrored video, fractured, building, damaging, appreciating, filling. One time I did too much ketamine & had to walk home K-holing. The hole thinks, wow, you are stupid. Degrading hole which has no master. The hole as hive-mind, as mutating, spreading virus. Hole changing with time. I could talk all day about holes. Debt is a hole. Fate is a hole. Morality is a hole. My love is a hole. A hole in a log grows moss, in my memory, more often than not. For the hole everything is good, so I must try to be more like the hole. Everything has its own hole. Enter me—a holy thing, as it pulls you deeper upon itself.

BROKEN CLAW

Trance like
        gelid frost on
windowpane which

            bows itself with time

    direct
        an eye towards
                translucence
            & become
illuminated by

THE WORST MEAL I EVER ATE / JEANNE D'ARC

LUNCH WAS A SAD MELTED FISH STICK / & SOME FRENCH FRIES / BOGGED TOGETHER / NOW WE ARE IN THE SHIT / I HEARD YESTERDAY THAT IF YOU MENTION GUN RESTRICTIONS IN NASHVILLE / OR IF YOU TALK ABOUT ABORTION / IN NORTH CAROLINA / THEY TIE YOU TO A STAKE / BLOOD VESSELS ARE ON THE VERGE OF BURSTING WHEN UPSIDE DOWN ABOVE A FLAME / SKIN CAN MELT TOO / OF COURSE / OR SAND TO GLASS / WHICH FORMS THE CEILING / ABOVE YOUR MATTRESS / & THROUGH THE NIGHT & THROUGH THE GLASS / A WEEPING WIND / WHICH KEEPS THE FLAME AT BAY / THE BURNING BECOME / A LOW SMOLDER / YOU FOUGHT FOR IT I CAN SAY THAT AT LEAST / BUT MY VISIONS / ARE YOUR VISIONS / & WHEN I TAKE THE STAND / I WILL LIE / & SAY I AM NOT A PROPHET / & THAT I DO NOT REMEMBER ANY OF MY DREAMS.

GUNK 2

Polluted wet dust
drying shitstain
empty head
apple rot
sunmelted tar
roof with melt
slush slop gross
excrement like
oil fields & drill
like fruit fly
floating
vile
unright
-eous

LUNCH

a can of flies in my cupboard a can a can of flies I live off a can of
flies they buzz & buzz & I live off a can of flies the little bastards
little little bastards get larvae & maggots in bread in coffee
grounds laid eggs in my bed laid eggs laid eggs in skin laid eggs
burrowed larvae maggots flies I can't live off a can off a can of flies
I can't live I can't live off a can of flies I can tlive ca ntlive c antlive
can't alive off a can of flies can't alive can't alive a life in a can of
flies I am burrowed in the mucus & debris of the flies I am looking
at the flies & in looking at the flies I am becoming the flies & in the
can can of flies I am becoming a can of flies hoarding the dense
muck that

        surrounds   us.

LANDKILL

If only because of
hovering halos
this ecstasy boils my halos
of their own boiling creosote the
sunning sheer of your face
sunning sheer of your veil
smiling sheer of your veil
your evil veil

if only in humming the tune to
Chopin's *Nocturne in C Sharp Minor*

if only by the goodwill of this fucking
nocturnal hellish
darkened & lightening & hungry flesh
if I am alive if I am alive if I am alive

if I am alive then there are seedlings
born from breaking
I pull over my face a laced fabric
opaquely deathly angelic dynamism
kills the boredom that is inside my skull
my love for you is a drench

& if only by going through the weeds
& if only going through controlled
burning controlled burning which leaves
the roots all black & bramble & brackish

& if only by the exiting of night
if only by the shouting of night
if only the washing waves
if only the opaque cloud

if only by breathing this likening
if only by exhaling the gasoline fume
if only by extraperiphery or by
crowning my face with varicosity
if dilating this circle
if dilating this circle
if dilating this circle
if dilating this circle

PATINA

Cutting through mandible excursion
hunting through tooth & exit
exiting through hunt & tooth
drastic in insurrection
drastic in interruption
crevasse of maw-like density
my air is draconian able-bodied
& untrustworthy tempting an
air draconian dragon-like flight
upon pedagogical destinies
which much like a sliver of silver
-painted silverware glistens
& gleams in every light

A DAY IN THE PARK

I

PULL THE CAMERA
THROUGH YOUR POCKET PULL THE
PULL THE CAMERA THROUGH YOUR POCKET
LOOK AROUND LOOK AROUND LOOK AROUND
LIKE YOUR LIFE DEPENDS ON IT
LOOK AROUND MY GOD ISN'T
IT ALL SO DISGUSTING & GORGEOUS YOU ARE
BECOMING THE THING YOU LOVE
TO BE BECOMING

II

SMOKE FROM THE COFFEE MUG SMOKE FROM
FROM THE COFFEE MUG MAKING MY INSIDES WEAK
MAKES MY INSIDES SICK & DIRTY WITH
MUCKY GUM LIKE ACID MADE MY EYES
DRY UNTIL I COULD NOT WEEP

III

& IN THE SUNSET WE ATE WHAT WE THOUGHT
WERE BERRIES BUT REALLY TURNED OUT TO BE
ANTS THAT CRAWL OVER YOUR SKIN GIVING IT A
TEXTURE A SHEEN WHERE YOUR SKIN SHOULD BE
A SHEEN WHERE YOUR SKIN SHOULD BE
WHAT WE FOUND WAS MUCH MORE DELICIOUS

CROWN SONNETS FOR SHOUTING

I

Bit by bit I enter the world

piece by piece by piece by piece

dripping with sap & boiling gunk

like floating vomit in the sink

the face of my watch is cracked

nothing but dead numbers

space by space my entry bores

into the holes my happiness built

the holes that my happiness built

adjacent ugliness of lonely chapels

our love is god & other things

are not so I turn my cage

I turn my cage to the cliffs

plank by plank I build my bridge

II

plank by plank I build   my bridge
plank plank plank plank plank plank
plank plank plank plank plank plank
plank plank plank plank plank plank
plank plank plank plank plank plank
plank plank plank plank plank plank
plank plank plank plank plank plank
plank plank plank plank plank plank
plank plank plank plank plank plank
plank plank plank plank plank plank
plank plank plank plank plank plank
plank plank plank plank plank plank
plank plank plank plank plank plank
plank by plank I build   my bridge

III

plank by plank I build my bridge
in one slow swing I cut the rope

burn the moldy rope the bridge
gets cut I cut the rope the rope to the bridge

I've left that gleaming gold place
sap-drip cuts holes in glass over time

to the bridge that I cut the rope to
the bridge I cut the rope to I apologize

to the bridge I cut the rope to my lifeline
adrift adrift adrift adrift

adrift my angry ocean lies in wait
adrift my angry ocean lies in wait like

placid tenderly lying in the sun
my angry ocean still for now

IV

my angry ocean still for now
my angry ocean still for now
my angry ocean still for now
my angry ocean still for now
my angry ocean still for now
my angry ocean still for now
my angry ocean still for now
my angry ocean still for now
my angry ocean still for now
my angry ocean still for now
my angry ocean still for now
my angry ocean still for now
my angry ocean still for now
my paper crown is lost at sea

V

my paper crown is lost at sea
my empty bridge a hollow door my
room returned to gunk or an ashtray
spilled in the corner in the dusty
corner in the dusty corner which has
                              no light

I turn to the gross mold I said I never would
turn to the gross mold again I said never again
I never said again that I would turn to the
mold in the window over the angry ocean's
roar which stands over the angry ocean
on occasion I walk down there to the ocean
& the ocean takes me & the ocean leaves
illusions born from tachyon psychosis

VI

illusions born from tachyon psychosis
illusions born from tachyon psychosis
illusions born from tachyon psychosis
illusions born from tachyon psychosis

illusions born from tachyon psychosis
illusions born from tachyon psychosis
illusions born from tachyon psychosis
illusions born from tachyon psychosis

illusions born from tachyon psychosis
illusions born from tachyon psychosis
illusions born from tachyon psychosis
illusions born from tachyon psychosis

illusions born from tachyon psychosis
bit by bit I enter the world

BEFORE WE EAT THE RAT — FIFTH WHEEL
PRESS, "DREAMLAND" ANTHOLOGY
DIGGING — BULLSHIT LIT ONLINE FEATURE

ACKNOWLEDGEMENTS

SPECIAL

THANKS

TO

LINDSAY HARGRAVE

VERONICA BENNETT

JAMES MINNIS

DEDICATED

TO

SILENCE

POSTSCRIPT

GOLIATH

BLASTING ARMAGEDDON COMES
FROM DERANGED SHADOWFIGURES WHICH
                    IN THE DARK SWIM.
AN ARDENT FACE   GLARES AT ME
FROM WHERE   THERE IS SURE   TO BE NO FACE.
& ALWAYS   THE WIND   OF WHISPER. CODDLE
OR CLAW, YOU HAVE NO CHOICE   BUT TO LISTEN.
I HEAR THE VOICES   OF WHICH YOU ALL SPEAK.
MY BREATH   A SENSE OF EXTREMITY. MY VISION
THE FUTURE.   I SEE WHAT   YOU DO NOT,   FOUL DEVIL.
MY INVERSE   IS YOUR INVERSE.   DIVEST EXCISE
DISTORT   EXHALE   DISTORT,   CABLE TELEVISION
HAS   NOTHING   ON   THIS.   TEMPERMENT LIKE
GLOWING CACTUS THORN.   DISTORTED WORLD.
          DISTORTED WORLD.   ALWAYS & FOREVER
DISTORTED WORLD.   MINE, YOURS, OURS.
IT BELONGS   TO ITSELF & I AM   JUST HERE
TO SEE THE SIGHTS.   STRAP MY
DEATHLY HAZE TO PILLARED   CUFFS,
WIELD   AN UNREAL   WEAPON:
                              PARANORMALITY
TAPPED   WITHIN DISCOVERY,   DOUSED IN GASHES.
I SEE   & SCREAM   FROM THE   PILLORY
I AM STRAPPED INTO THE PILLORY
          I AM BURNED ALIVE.
WHEN I DIE   MY VOICE   CARRIES ON
          INTO THE BODY OF ANOTHER.

I HAVE SEEN IT WITH MY BLOODIED BEATING EYES
THE GOLIATH, COME TO TAKE ME,
STANDING UPON ETERNITY & ALL
OF CONSCIOUS THOUGHT. THE GOLIATH
IS TOWERING. GOLIATH TOWERING OPIOIDS.
GOLIATH TOWERING LIKE OTHER
SORTS OF PHARMACEUTICALS. GOLIATH A LONG
IRON CAST SHADOW ACROSS DEMONS OF GUILT.
            DEVIL! DEVIL I HEAR YOUR
UPROAR OF PANDEMONIOUS GOLIATHS
YOUR POUTING NORMALCY BOREDOM
INVOCATIONS HALLUCINATIONS EXPERIENCES
WITH THE AETHER VISION OF WALLS FALLING
AWAY & NOTHING LEFT BUT
BLANK SPACE & THE WHISPERING,
THE WHISPERING OF THE GOLIATH,
LARGE MOUTH. USED TO THINK IT WAS
GOD I SPOKE TO NOW I KNOW
IT IS SOMETHING ELSE EQUALLY REAL.
I CANNOT TELL WHETHER IT CREATED ME
OR OTHERWISE. I CANNOT TELL IF IT
DETERMINES MY ACTIONS OR OTHERWISE,
OR OTHERWISE, OR OTHERWISE. MY DESPERATION
FOR YOUR CONNECTION, MY HALLUCINATION
OF YOUR HAND IN MY HAND, MY HEAD
WEIGHTED IN THE OTHER, WEEPING;
THIS IS A VISION I GRIEVE. WHAT IS REAL IS THE SAME
AS WHAT IS UNREAL & IT IS ALSO EQUALLY GOOD.
THERE IS INHERENCE, THERE IS COMMUNICATION.
I CAN HEAR YOUR THOUGHTS. SOMETIMES,
THEY TELL ME TO LEAVE. OTHER TIMES,
THEY TELL FLOWERPETAL YELLOW GHOSTING

SMOKE-LIKE VAPOROUS SYNTHESIS, SLOWLY MOVING
THE SECOND-HAND OF A CLOCK, SLOWLY,
                    SLOWLY,
          SLOWLY.
GOLIATH O DO NOT BEAR DOWN UPON ME
                         WITH YOUR HAND,
VULNERABILITY AS ANTIDOTE,
               KNIFE-BLADE AS SERRATED
                    BANDAGE.
MY VISION OF YOU AS
THE PHARMACEUTICALS BEGIN TO HIT,
& NOW I AM HERE, IN THE SHIT, WITHOUT YOU,
JUST LIKE I WAS BEFORE.
MY INSTINCT IS THAT YOU UNDERSTAND ME,
NOT THAT IT MATTERS. MY LIFE SAVINGS
IS A BUCKET OF QUARTERS
& A BROKEN SILVER DOLLAR BASKET OF
                         FORGET-ME-NOTS,
& MY BODY IS ONE OF THEM,
A PETAL-LIKE BLOSSOM INEXTRICABLE
                    FROM ALL THINGS.

www.ingramcontent.com/pod-product-compliance
Lightning Source LLC
Chambersburg PA
CBHW061327120626
46546CB00007B/2708